SWALLOWTAIL

SWALLOWTAIL

poems by

Brenna Twohy

Published by Button Poetry / Exploding Pinecone Press

Minneapolis, MN 55403 | http://www.buttonpoetry.com

WHEN I SAY I FORGIVE YOU, KNOW THIS

I did not bury the hatchet.
I have the hatchet in my hands.
I am building myself a new house.

CONTENTS

SWALLOWTAIL

I GUESS I'LL TELL IT LIKE THIS

did you know
sand dollars grow heavier skeletons

in rough water?
& did you know

young sand dollars can't
make themselves heavy enough, so

they eat pebbles
to weigh their bodies down?

& did you know
the things that I have swallowed

just to keep this body
safe from the current?

& did you know
when I say *the current*

I mean
this body

& did you know
there is a man

I can only talk about in metaphor,
the way his tattoos make

an avalanche of my mouth
(even now)

& did you know
there are whole years

I have dropped
to the bottom of an uneasy ocean

& did you know
this is how we evolve?

Hunted girls
grow shells

& they call us
hard women.

As if survival
could ever be delicate.

As if we haven't been chewing
rocks for generations.

As if we haven't been rebuilding
our own bones.

THREE TRUE THINGS ABOUT THE MAN
FROM THAT LAST POEM

His favorite fruit is the kiwi,
but when I asked him
he forgot, said pineapple,
woke days later, realizing his mistake.

& you should have heard his poems,
the way his arms pulsed to imaginary symphonies,

I called his mouth an orchestra.
When he smoked, I swear, he was a whole ballet.

He winked at me once, so I took a train south,
not wanting to gamble what would happen
should he close both eyes at once.
& when he did,

it was a weeknight. was my half-birthday,
not that I'd noticed at the time,
or would have done anything
differently if I had,
kissing him with all my yes,
not knowing about the next part,

how
     I
would
     let
him
     zip
my
     dress
up
     after.

how it was the gentlest of guttings.
how I did not ever say the word *no*.

how my mouth did not belong to me.
how I walked the nine miles home.
how every dog I passed
was barking.

how I did not then know what to call it,
so I called it nothing.

& woke years later,

realizing the mistake.

TO THE GUY IN THE BACK OF THE ROOM COMPLAINING ABOUT READING ANOTHER RAPE POEM

I get it.
I know you are tired of hearing rape poems.

I am tired of hearing rape poems,
the same way soldiers are tired
of hearing their own guns go off.

We all wish the war was over. But
you are staring out at a world on fire
complaining about how ugly
you think the ashes are.

The poems are not the problem.

We have built cathedrals
out of spite and splintered bone,
of course they aren't pretty,
nothing holy ever is—

Anita Hill over the shouting,
a crown of thorns plucked by men who
have never seen a blooming flower,
the sweat on your mother's sacred chest
as she pushed to get you here.

The work is never pretty,
but it's the only way the house gets built;
I know you don't want to look at my wreckage, but
I have carpentry in my mouth.
I have a hammer in my hands—
you cannot stop me from building.

& as long as you're there
in the back of the room,
I am going to be here,
voice made from smolder,
because this is my story
and you cannot take this
from me.

WHAT I'VE LEARNED ABOUT TRAUMA

It isn't as easy as being
      Something That Happened to You,
a package you opened once.

You will wake up in a new ZIP code,
      have to wander your way home,
carry a few of the things you love to this new place
      you live in now.

& so you buy throw pillows.
      You put up twinkle lights & have a big celebration,

point at the open windows
      & tell everyone who has ever seen you crying—

      look.
      look how I have not caged myself.
      look what I have made out of two paint buckets
      and the blessing of my still-here body.

but, of course,
      trauma leans into the bar cart.

Spills a drink on the new rug.
      Breaks off the door handle on his way out.
Trauma sends you letters
      without warning
for the rest of your life,
      usually disguised as something else—

a medical bill, maybe,
      or a box of photo albums packaged up by your father,

just so you remember
        trauma knows exactly where you live—

who did you think built the house?

THE PEACHES SHRIVEL ON THE COUNTER,
refusing to make themselves into jam.

what an insolent woman I have become.
knowing exactly how sweet I am
on a hungry man's tongue,
& handing him the stone of me.

peach pits are poisonous.
this is not a mistake.
girlhood is growing fruit
around cyanide. it will never be

yours for the swallowing.

SHELL GAME

The magician places three shells on a table, then hides a ball underneath one. He moves the shells around, then asks which has the ball underneath.

I.

We got the turtle one December in the mid-nineties, when we all got jammies Christmas Eve & Santa brought the tree down the chimney. He had dark orange patterns on his shell and a tiny black Sharpie dot on his underside that I marked there one afternoon, a selfish secret. We built him a box in the backyard; fed him carrots & took him out to crawl up and down our arms. We named him Hector, after the man who gave him to us, my Nana's boyfriend, a man with a strong laugh and the same three jokes.

I don't know how long Hector (the turtle) was gone, the first time, before we noticed the empty box.

II.

The magician is using more than one ball.

III.

It wasn't until a decade later I found out from my Nana what Hector (the man) had done to her.

The way their home became a box she didn't know her way out of.

IV.

You will never guess the correct shell.

This is the way the game is designed.

V.

I found Hector (the turtle) like two years later, knew him from the dot on the bottom of his shell. He crawled into my hands like he'd never been gone.

The first time I left, I came back within the week.

& I don't like to talk about this part.

The way I told my friends   *it's going to be better*
as I fit myself back inside my shell.

I know a thing or two about legacy.

VI.

The magician shows you there's nothing under the shell you pointed to, then lifts it again to reveal the ball beneath, transported.

VII.

& what am I now if not an empty shell? I thought as my phone started to ring. On the other end, my favorite voice & the same three apologies.

This is how we learn staying.

VIII.

This is the way the game is designed.

IX.

When he finally stopped singing   *come home,*

I was not relieved.

There is more than one way a heart can break.

X.

I'm trying to be better about forgiveness. & this, too, is a slow and painful
unpacking,

      the shedding of so many unneeded shells.

SWALLOWTAIL

The medical history form reads, "Has someone physically, sexually, or emotionally abused you?" with a box for yes and a box for no.

☐   I am mostly fine

☐   I am mostly fine but

☐   One Thanksgiving his mom told me this story about how as a child he found a butterfly in the yard with half a wing missing. He cupped it in his hands, brought it inside, and held it covered against his stomach for fear it would fly away. They called the animal hospital on the landline and were instructed to carefully clip the healthy wing to match the broken one.

☐   A cage of gentle
hands is still a cage,
and I know this now.

☐   I would have climbed in the jar if he'd asked me.
I would have torn the good wing off myself.

JANUARY

May

It has been a year since the last time I told him I loved him,
and it scratches at the back of my throat,
a nasty cough desperate to break free from my body.

My horoscope reads,
"Happy Birthday, Gemini!
Mercury is retrograde
and didn't buy you a present.
The planets didn't think you'd make it.
We watched you collect pill bottles
and we settled in for a long winter.
We saw you pacing on that bridge
and the whole sky dressed in black."

April

I'm worried you're biting off more than you can chew,

everyone says,
and I laugh
and run my tongue hard
against the sharps of my teeth.

Look into my mouth.
This endless, angry thing.
You have no idea how much I can consume.

March

I read an article about
the Instinctive Drowning Response.
It doesn't look anything
like in the movies—

you don't call for help.
Just try to pull air into your lungs.
Just try to survive this water.
Sometimes a child will go under
while their parent is watching,
and they don't even know anything is
wrong.

My mom asks if everything's okay,
and I say, *Of course.*

Drowning is a quiet, desperate thing.

February

Three dozen crows drop dead
in downtown Portland
and no one knows why.

January

One time in junior high we found a 24-pack of Natty Light
stuck up in a tree in that field with the water tower.
It was at least a hundred degrees that whole summer,
and we sipped skunky sun-scorched beer and thought,
This is the life.

One time I wrote in my notebook,
*He loves me so much
it might shatter me,*

which tastes different
now.

ON SEEING PHOTOS OF HIS NEW GIRLFRIEND ON FACEBOOK

I call her Rebecca.
Give her a tabby cat
and the perfect voice for folk songs.

Call her Julie.
Call her a new windowpane
in the space of
all that shattered glass.
I give her a root cellar
(because of course
she has a root cellar),

I call her Heather. Call her
a sturdy rope swing
made from the old noose.

Last night I bought the wrong cereal
and hated myself
out of nostalgia.

I bet she is an excellent grocery shopper.
I bet she rides one of those bicycles with the basket
and likes the taste of whiskey.
I bet she uses a DivaCup
and never spills anything on her fingers.

I wonder about her fingers,
if they've ever raked through
the dry dirt of her twenties
until they bled.

Surely
something must be growing here,
right?

Because otherwise
how do you forgive yourself
for your rotting?
At least
I still have my name.

At least
he left me

that.

THE FISHERMAN TAKES THE FISH HOME & TELLS HER HE LOVES HER

I.

A magician talks about the record for holding one's breath
as his assistant lowers herself into a tank of water.

He calls it twenty-two minutes, but I swear to you it's longer.
I swear to you, it's years.

II.

This is how I remember it:

On our first date,
he ran his fingertips across my skin like he was reading my palm.

When I fell asleep with my glasses on, he slid them off
and cleaned them, then placed them on my nightstand.
Every single time.

Once, I took a sip of wine,
shrugged, and set my glass down on the counter.
He poured it down the sink. Then the entire bottle.
He said, *Life is too short for bad wine.*

He said, *You deserve better.*

III.

God, I love doing magic tricks.

I love the way I know the lie from the beginning.
I love the way I can see the turn coming.

IV.

This is the hardest part:

That boy is not made of fists.

That boy learned how to braid my hair.

These things do not untruth themselves
when the first door slams.

I did not stop loving him
all the months I was holding my breath.

This is the hardest part:

The way a fish is still a fish
even after she's been gutted.

Even after her lip's split clean in half
from the hook
       and the hook
             and the hook.

Do you think the fish blames herself?
And her own stupid, open mouth?

Do you think the fisherman apologized?

Said all he wanted was to hold her? Said,

I've touched that hook for years and it never once pierced me,
       darling, how could I have known?

Do you think the fish forgave him? Said,

I'm sorry, too.
I promise I'll try harder
to breathe outside the water.

WHEN HE TELLS THE STORY

he cracks a joke about
dodging a bullet.

When I tell the story,
there is still a bullet. Finally done

kissing the gun on his mouth.

ON KISSING THE NEXT BOY

I had forgotten the way
a man's mouth can
be only his mouth

& not an overdue apology

or a staircase
between two unmoving doors

can you taste him I do not ask

the way
he heated water on the stovetop
when my bath ran cold

the way I loved him
exactly the wrong amount

just enough to wreck me
but not enough to stay

the way I kissed him
for the last time
like the outbreath on a sucker punch

like an undone whistle

CONSIDER THIS YOUR ONLY WARNING

On nights my body feels
more cage than shelter

& my hands ache from the rebuilding,
I paint my lipstick on extra thick

& go out searching for men
with eyes like hunters.

They see the way I smolder,
& they think *whiskey* & they think *easy,*

not knowing I have swallowed hell
& carried it back in my belly.

Sometimes I call this healing.
Sometimes I twist my hair up,

cross my legs, & watch them
learn the difference

between a smile
& the baring of teeth.

COLFAX

Walking home[1]
I play the voicemail again,[2]
and again[3]
and then I do the dishes
and get into bed.[4]

––––––––––––––––

1. past the bar where I turned twenty-two,
    the bar where we fought about the right way
    to tie a cherry stem with your tongue
    which is, of course,
    to leave it in the glass

2. & I like to think I'm three years smarter,
    but I'm just three years used
    to the way you wink
    when you say anyone's name

3. look, I wouldn't be lying
    if I said you know me best of anyone,
    but that truth
    is my least favorite thing about me

4. & not being there is
    the kindest thing
    you have ever done.

I SWORE I WOULDN'T DO THIS AGAIN,

use magic as metaphor,
call this heart anything more
than what she is: a fool
who's forgotten every trapdoor
she's ever been led softly into.

but I do this trick;
learned it from my grandfather, where
I pass you two face-up Aces & tell you to
hold them tightly as you can
between two flat palms.

one night in early August, I dreamt
we built a cabin in the Catskills.

if the bartender looked over,
she might mistake it for a prayer.
your pressed-together hands.
the way the devil keeps his distance.

here, let me spoil this quickly:
you're holding both jokers &
we haven't been in this bar
for months now. you drink
your Jameson in a different city.

see how easy that was?

I might have wished you
more honest, but then

what would we have had in common?

back in the bar, I lean to kiss you halfway
through a story about the chickenpox.

this is not the first time
I've built a cabin.

there was a house
where we kept all the pasta
in big mason jars on the counter.

there was a house
where I spilled grapefruit juice
and no one yelled.

in some version of this story, you do not
slip a future into my pressed-together palms
and ask me to guess the thing between them.

but meanwhile, at that bar,
your fingertips are all lined up.
I've practiced years to make this part
look easy. like I've done nothing.

like I could do this same trick
again and again and again.

HE HAS ANOTHER WOMAN'S NAME
TATTOOED ON THE INSIDE OF HIS LEFT WRIST

& this, too, beckons me to him
like flame to an already-collapsing church,
all his holy haloing above us as we tell fortunes
in the tea leaf patterns of our smolder,
& goddamn if it doesn't feel like worship.

I have a ring that he did not give me
bundled in a pair of socks at the back of my bottom drawer,
& when I cannot sleep, I take it out & wear it.

& it is not a promise, but a photograph
of a woman I ended up not turning into.

her name might be my favorite part of his body,
the ugly honesty of it, the way it lays bare
the exact contours of someone else's scarring.

I trace the letters with my best kind of gentle, tell him,

> *I love every person*
> *who has ever loved you well.*

paint this on my skin—

blessed be the flood that brings forth the garden.
blessed be those who have left me undone
and reaching.

SOMEONE LIVES
IN APARTMENT FOUR.

I know it because I've heard her fucking.

packages with her name appear and disappear off the porch.
one whole week her snow boots were left drying by the vents.

she likes to time her fucking,
ensuring it begins twenty to forty minutes after I have fallen asleep,
and lasts until I have contemplated setting a small fire
both to force an evacuation (and a presumptive end to the fucking)
but also in retaliation for the reminder
my own bed has never been such a showy symphony.

I know she lives there
despite never having seen her
the same way I know the promise
nothing will change between us
has been quietly and unceremoniously broken.

saying we have not become strangers by the distance
does as much good as saying apartment four is empty.

(believe me, I know about the word empty
and the many meanings it can bear.)

there is no one to blame for this but the both of us.

I never put my boots by the vents and now
it's April and they are dripping wet

TOUCHDOWN JESUS

It will take you eight minutes to drive through the entirety of La Cañada Flintridge, which accounts for you hitting all three traffic lights & for the full two minutes you will spend pulled over in the parking lot of the Lutheran church staring up at Touchdown Jesus. Touchdown Jesus is like four stories tall and carved entirely of marble. Touchdown Jesus is where we will meet you before the party. someone will bring a bottle of whipped cream vodka & someone will bring a Costco pack of Mike's Hard & someone will give someone else a blowjob like four feet away & someone will be holding my hand as we run from the cops through the too-warm night like fear is something we have any right to—

listen, this whole town is a friend you do not want
                                    staying with you when they come to visit.

listen, one day all the swimming pools in all the neighborhoods will forget how to float you. listen, one time they found a colony of bees swarming in Touchdown Jesus's ear & then the church told us it had never been Jesus at all, it had been Touchdown Paul the whole time, & the entire town is like this.

they will only claim you until something in your head starts
buzzing. until something poison nests itself inside of you.

listen, I consider myself a pretty good kid but the last time I saw my brother alive we were getting high together in an alley ten minutes before family dinner

& I do not know why I am telling you this except to say
                                    I have loved a man who had a swarm inside of him.

or
                                    the day he died I watched all the world's honey dissolve
                                                into a bee's mouth.

or back home there is this hollow, buzzing body that was holy until it wasn't, which is what we do to you in this town; but one time my parents bought us a snow cone machine & we set it up on the street corner & I'm not certain, but I think it might still be there & if this whole town is a lesson on escape, I am a nest

or a hive

or a swarm
bumping up against the edges of an eardrum

and calling it the entire world.

SPOILER ALERT

I.

I was snooping in mom's jewelry box
when I found the teeth
jumbled up in a folded envelope
that rattled like a pack of Chiclets when
I shook it.

II.

When my brother came home
with his first tattoo,
mom laid the spoon carefully
across the top of the simmering pot,
then opened the leftmost drawer
& pulled out the cheese grater,
only half-joking about scraping it
off his skin.

(Spoiler alert: The brother in this story is dead now.)

III.

I opened the envelope
just enough to peek inside.

Are these mine?
All of yours, she said.

All my babies' baby teeth.

IV.

When we would play hide & seek,
I went for the same spot each time.

There was this tiny door
in the middle of my wall that
led to a laundry hamper &
a door on the other side
leading to mom & dad's room.

I would pile dirty clothes
onto myself & hide
there, an unwashed thing.

(Spoiler alert: The me in this story is dead now.)

V.

He sent me a text ten days before he died
& I did not respond to it.

& I have not forgiven this.

VI.

I asked why I was the only one
in the family with green eyes.

Those are your baby eyes,
my brothers said. *One day they'll*
fall out and your grown-up eyes
will come in.

VII.

My first Christmas back from college,
he took all of the Xanax from my purse.

& I have not forgiven this.

VIII.

Once when I was four or five, mom
found me asleep in the hamper
hours later, waiting
to be found.

IX.

I used to wiggle my teeth until they bled,
then cry about the bleeding.   I thought I
would have more time
to tell these stories.   Even
the ones that split my gums. Even when
they came in crooked & eventually
I yanked them out.

I don't know
what to do with these sharp
& mouthless memories,

this envelope of loose teeth.

THERE'S THIS STORY MOM TELLS

about these gorgeous tomato plants
she was growing in the front yard.
how I plucked each of them—green
and hardened—from the vine, piled them
in my wheelbarrow, dragged them into the kitchen,
showed her how I had helped, asked if she was proud

& she could not bring herself
to tell me what I had done.

there are these dreams I've been having
where your body is our front yard.
where our family is this barren vine.
where I am so much
wailing, unripe fruit.

you've been gone three months exactly, so
I tell strangers about the costume contest.

how I was little red riding hood.
how you rushed the stage,
gentle wolf. playful snarl.
how you carried me the whole way home.

I have a wheelbarrow mouth.

I drag your name with me
everywhere I go.

A COWORKER ASKS ME IF I AM SAD, STILL

& I tell her,

grief is not a feeling
but a neighborhood.

this is where I come from.
everyone I love still lives there.

someday I hope to raise a family
in a place you could not mistake
for any home I've ever been in.

Brenna, she says,
>   *there's no such thing*
>   *as an unhaunted house.*

MONDEGREEN

In 1997, three days before my mother's birthday, Chumba-
wamba releases the iconic *Tubthumping*, & everyone I know
spends the next ten years trying to unremember it, but de-
spite our best efforts, any time we walk into a Red Robin or
a Spencer's Gifts, we will all sing along loudly: *I get knocked
down, but I get up again, you're never gonna keep me down,*
with the notable exception of my brother, who will sing just
as loudly: *I get knocked down, but I can opera sing, and I'm
never gonna lose my voice.*

It's called a mondegreen, a misheard lyric, like how the
Ramones will sing, *I wanna be sedated,* & my mom will nod
along as she sings, *I want a piece of bacon.* It's the way our
brains fill in gaps, make sense of things we didn't
         or couldn't hear, the way my mom said,
he's gone, & I asked her   *where?*

I could not make sense of it, even though I had played this
song for a decade, lip-syncing the chorus every time my
phone rang in the middle of the night, & still I did not recog-
nize it when it played.

My brother had a compass with each of our names tattooed
on his chest, & on the plane my mom said, *I want to have
that, you know.* & of course she meant the compass.
                    But I thought she meant his skin.

A person who used to be me wrote a poem that same morn-
ing, & now I do not understand the words, or the conversa-
tions of anyone who did not know him, never played him in
dominos or listened for the sound of his breathing across
a hallway and two closed doors. Spring has come so early
I must be mishearing it. We clean out his trailer & there is
nothing there to make sense of:

an unopened bag of Swedish Fish. & the space where they found his body. The last thing he sent his friend Alex was a quote from a poem I wrote years ago about how difficult it was to love him. A poem that let both of us shout the wrong words.

I cannot edit out the wound I sang into us. But I can promise *I'm never gonna lose my voice.*

NEVILLE LONGBOTTOM'S BOGGART ATTENDS SEVERUS SNAPE'S FUNERAL

& no one will look directly at him.
even though he is in the front row.
even though he's the biggest thing in the room.
the whole world pulls a handkerchief from her pocket
and whispers the word *redemption*.
and the boggart stares into the casket,
wonders what it feels like
to wash a dead man's hands clean.

& of course, it is a tragedy—
that you name your abuser,

finally,
in a room full of people,
and they shrug, tell you of a girl he loved once,

lecture you about forgiveness, about changing spots
on the leopards that are still hunting you,

pretend they weren't watching
as your trauma
wrapped itself in your grandmother's clothes
and dared you to survive it loudly.

remember, this is a story about a boy who lives.

about power
that does not come easy,
the magic of packed earth
and the things that dare
to come out of it.

let your courage
make a mess of their story.
let it crawl into his coffin

ugly
and thumping
and unburied.

IN WHICH I DO NOT FEAR HARVEY DENT

The best part of having superpowers
is that most of the time
other people do not even know that you have them.

Like the days that I get out of bed
and put on appropriate workplace attire
and eat three meals, none of which are Hot Pockets,
people can't even tell that right then,
at that moment,
I am using my superpowers.

Anxiety is your body's response to perceived danger
and mine is so strong
you would have to call it a superpower.

It never gives up,
it is always looking for a fight,
it is the fiercest part of me.

When Rogue found out what her touch could do
to anyone who got close to her,
she crafted herself a costume
to keep anyone from ever touching her skin.

After I did not die
for the second time,
I learned how to make this urgent flame
look like a lantern.

How to make this hurricane alarm
come out like a poem.

If you think I am brave
it is because you have never seen me out of costume,
would not even recognize me outside of this armor.
I know what my touch can do to the people close to me,

to the lover who said, *I just can't handle you
when you get like this.*

There is a reason panic attacks
are not called panic fair fights.

They will come for you when you are sleeping.
When you are in the grocery store.
When you are making love with someone
and it could not be more perfect,

they are the worst kind of villain,
creeping in unnoticed until you are surrounded,
until you cannot imagine
any superpower that could ever overcome it,
until you have to explain to the doctor,
*It's not that I have a mental illness,
it's just that I have trouble breathing
when I leave my house.*

I have spent years just like Spider-Man, convinced
the best way to protect the people who loved me
was to leap from a tall building. The worst part
of having superpowers is that most of the time
other people do not even know that you have them.

This heavy thing
your body was not built to hold.

But if you think I am brave,
just wait until you see me out of costume.

I know what it is to fight monsters.

I know how strong an ordinary human has to be.

THAT AWFUL MONTH I CAN
ONLY WRITE POEMS ABOUT LEAVING,
AND/OR ABOUT LIMP BIZKIT

I.

What I need you to know about The Leaving
is that it feels like a toddler's art project—
something done messily
with clumsy, filthy hands.

Everyone will tell you how impressive it all is,
and how proud you should be,
as they place their clean palms to their unbruised chests
and stick The Leaving up on the fridge.

And you will pack everything you own
into eleven boxes you stole from the back of the grocery store
and move into a new house
where you still flinch every time you hear a door open,
even if you are the one opening the door,
and you will stare at this muddle of paint
that is the rest of your life, and wonder—
What the fuck is this even supposed to be?

II.

Months later,
immediately after breaking down in the urgent care lobby
when you realize
"name of emergency contact"
is a question you no longer know the answer to,
Limp Bizkit will come on the radio,
and somehow everything will be so much worse
than it was before the biscuit was limp,
and the child in the chair across from you will start screaming
and covering her ears, which seems entirely appropriate

given the circumstances, and you know
this image would have made him laugh for hours,
and for a moment it is like he is right there,
and you will smile
until your cheekbone starts to ache
and you check the mirror
for bruising.

III.

I haven't cooked chicken in four months.

The meat thermometer ended up in one of his boxes,
and I have never been able to tell just by looking
when something is finished.

I have terrible instincts about what is unsafe.

This is not a metaphor.
I am really afraid of food poisoning, and I know
given an oven and enough time
I would cook the chicken until it was charred and crumbling,

and this is not a metaphor.
This is not about the way my mother
taught me to check if meat was done
by stabbing my knife into the thickest part,
not about how I didn't hear the timer go off
until the entire kitchen was on fire.

He seemed like such a nice guy, everyone says,
as I tell them my new address,

as if you can tell from outside an oven
if the meat inside is poison.

IV.

I used to imagine all the time what his ex-wife thought about me.
And she never knew my name. Had no idea
the way I climbed inside his body
and convinced myself it was a place I could live in,
but I thought of her constantly,
a ghost that lived in our house.

The night we fought about leaving the lights on,
the night he threw the flour jar
and it exploded on the wall next to me,
I said I was sorry, went into the bathroom,
and saw my entire body covered in flour.

I look just like a ghost, I thought.
A ghost that lives in our house.

and I laughed
and I laughed
and I laughed

(ARIEL IS NOT THE FIRST URSULA'S MADE AN OFFER TO.)

My therapist tells me
I have Unresolved Issues

Related to Trusting Men,
which strikes me

as like telling a mermaid
she has Unresolved Issues

Related to Living on Dry Land.
We have felt the heat

of those things most likely to kill us
& decided not to leave

our bones there. We've been
promised the world

for our silence, & we
continue to sing.

THE PROBLEMS WITH FIRST DATES, OR
HOW TO REALLY REALLY REALLY NOT GET LAID

The first problem is that we are at Tony Roma's.

& don't get me wrong, I will eat the fuck out of some ribs,
but every person in this room looks exactly like my dad; &

the second problem is that I have not had sex
since the first *Twilight* movie came out, which means
a fictional Mormon girl has made out with a vampire,
made out with a werewolf, thrown herself off a cliff,
gone to Italy, gotten married, and had a demon baby
claw its way out of her vagina
since I last had an orgasm with another person in the room,

& now
there are a hundred of my dad
staring at me, slurping shrimp cocktail
and I need to say *something*.

Did you know that whales can only have sex in groups of three?

The third problem is that I just said,
Did you know that whales can only have sex in groups of three?

& he says   *what.*

& I say, *YES! Because they can't actually swim and fuck
at the same time, so a third whale comes along
to hold them aloft as they do it, like a blubbery sex table!*

The fourth problem is that when I drink too much,
I start thinking about a man
I haven't spoken to in two years.

I used to think being in love with someone meant
being the person they grow old at Tony Roma's with, but

being in love is so much easier from across a room.

Or a small town.
Or two years of radio silence,

& I sometimes wonder if this way of loving someone
is my best way of loving someone:
with miles and miles between us.

Like how you can still find the North Star every time—
you never wonder if it can pick you out of a crowd,
or if it still remembers all the words to the first Stones song
you ever danced to, you just want to be able to see it
from far away because you know if you got any closer,
odds are you'd catch on fire.

He has a wife now.

She has his last name. & a house with a fireplace.
& when she comes home from work
she goes to sleep in a bed that is Their Bed.

& three weeks after he cut his losses,
I traded our bed in for a single because
it felt more like a choice.

Like I was choosing to go to bed alone
rather than trying to sleep with the entire night sky next to me,
beckoning me to fall back into it,

because I lied
(before)
when I said it was easier to love someone from a distance.

It isn't easier.
It is just smaller.

More convenient to fit into a back pocket,
or a time capsule, or that place between the bed and the wall,
that place you're still afraid monsters will crawl out of,

like he left a piece of himself with you
and you are terrified he is coming back for it.

Or he left a piece of himself with you and you are terrified
he is not coming back for it.

The fifth problem is
when a new man tells you he likes you too much
already, it doesn't sound like a promise.

It sounds like a smoke alarm
warning you to get out fast—

If you hurry,
you might miss the worst of it.

FANTASTIC BREASTS AND WHERE TO FIND THEM

What turns me on is
Ginny Weasley in the Restricted Section with her skirt hiked up,
Sirius Black in a secret passageway
solemnly swearing he is up to no good,
Draco Malfoy in the Room of Requirement
Slytherin into my Chamber of Secrets.

I am an unapologetic consumer of all things Potterotica,
but the sexiest part is not the sound of Myrtle moaning,
the sexiest part is knowing she is part of a bigger story.

Don't give me raw meat
& tell me it is nourishment.
I know a slaughterhouse when I see one.

It looks like 24/7 live streaming
reminding me men are going to fuck me
whether I like it or not, that
there is one use for my mouth
and it is not speaking, that
a man is his most powerful
when he's got a woman by the hair.

The first time a man I loved
held me by the wrists and called me a whore,
I did not think,

Run.

I thought,

This is just like the movies.

I know a slaughterhouse when I see one.

It looks like websites and seminars
teaching you how to fuck more bitches;
looks like 15-year-old boys bullied for being virgins;

it looks like the man who did not flinch
when I said, *Stop*. And he heard, *Try harder*.

If you play-act at butchery long enough
you grow used to the sounds of the screaming.

It is just a side effect of industry;
everything gets cut into small, marketable pieces.
You can almost forget they were ever real bodies.

I will not practice bloody hands.
I will not make-believe dissected women.

My sex cannot be packaged,
my sex is *magic.*

It is part of a bigger story.
I am whole.
I exist
when you are not fucking me,
and I will not be cut into pieces
anymore.

HEY, JEFF PROBST!
I WANNA BE ON YOUR SHOW.

I wanna lay in hammocks and say shit like,
I'm not here to make friends,
because when I say that in my everyday life
people look at me like I am an unpleasant person
to be around.

Hey, Jeff Probst!
I like the parts where you have auctions
because that is like real-life eBay
or perhaps just like a regular auction,
I don't really know, I don't get out a whole lot.

Hey, Jeff Probst!
I do not like the part where you make them eat things
like alive snakes—let's please not do that on our season.

Jeff, two years ago,
a woman talked about her abuse
around your campfire.
After the commercial, a man said
he understood why her father had beaten her.

Said he would have done it too.

& you poured it into my living room, as easy as ratings.

To be an abuse survivor
is to be the worst kind of thirsty;
surrounded by water that will kill you if you drink it,
as everyone on the shoreline says,

Look
at all that
gorgeous ocean.

Jeff, when I left him,
he rented a U-Haul &
he moved me into my new house.

We fell asleep
on a twin mattress
on the concrete floor,

which is the softest name I have for drowning.

What do you know about saving yourself?
& all its wretched gasping?

What do you call womanhood
if not endurance? The ways we
withstand that which we did not
believe withstandable, and then
put our own holy hands to work.

Call me Survivor.
It is the ugliest triumph I own,
but it is mine.

It is mine.

WHAT I MEAN WHEN I SAY SURVIVOR

I, too,
have loved men
who named my mouth
ashtray,
mistook me for a place
to leave
burning things
when they were done.

LITTLE RED RIDING HOOD ADDRESSES
THE NEXT WOLF

You hear the story
of the horrors done to my body,
and you say,

> *We aren't all like that, you know.*
> *Let me show you how gentle my hands are.*

It's not your fault, you say,
that your teeth
are the same shape
as his teeth.

But I was swallowed whole
and they renamed me caution
for their daughters.
I was swallowed whole
and they said,

> *That is what happens*
> *to little girls who climb in bed with monsters.*

There are mornings
when my own bedroom
looks exactly like the middle of the woods.

& I'm not calling you dangerous.
I'm just making sure you understand
the moral of the story.

This has nothing to do with the threat
of strangers in the forest.

The moral of the story is
I will gut you if I need to.

I will carve my way out
using only my teeth.

CONVERSATIONS ABOUT TOP CHEF

after Desiree Dallagiacomo

So they take these 15 cooks, right? & they put them together in a kitchen & tell them to make a six-course meal out of vending machine snacks & then the judges say ridiculous shit, like, *I wonder if perhaps the Bugles would have made for a better taste contrast than the Doritos* & then everyone says, *I am not a pastry chef* & then everyone cooks scallops, like all the time, they are always cooking scallops, & then they have to make a wedding cake out of taco shells, & one time, when my brother Matt was like four years old, he went into the front yard & he sprinkled a packet of taco seasoning onto the soil there & he waited for the taco shells to grow, & my mom told him, *Buddy, there are some things that just don't grow here,* but the next morning, she woke at like 5 AM to go into the front yard & push six taco shells into the soft dirt there, & when he saw them, he said, *I knew!*

&
we
did
not
have
a funeral.

Just a barbecue. Just five jumbo bags of Cheetos & what was left of our family. & we did not bury his body. But if we had, I know, nothing would have grown there. You would not believe the amount of salt that most things need. Would not believe how hot you have to get a pan to get a good sear on. A week after he died, we found his Top Chef audition tape. He's holding a blood orange in his left hand as he cuts it with his right. We all watched breathless, not knowing where the knife would end up. I will never again not know the sound of my mother breaking. So I chew on tinfoil & I call it a meal. I chew on the gristle of the last time we talked on the phone & I do not think I will ever be ready to swallow it.

Tell me again about the part where grief is not my name.

I will tell you my parents have not kissed on the lips since the nineties. I will tell you there is so much I did not say out of respect for the living. I will tell you one of the first rules of working in a kitchen is

       you never try to catch a falling knife.

but lord,   if we didn't try anyhow.
lord,   if we aren't a family of good intentions

                        & cut off hands.

DRACO MALFOY
LOOKS INTO THE MIRROR OF ERISED

& the portraits fade from his mother's walls.
Narcissa sips Firewhiskey with a different man,
his hair dark and simple.

Maybe he has a mole on his jawline.
Maybe he has an accent only when he's been drinking.
Maybe they have a beautiful daughter
whose forearm bears nothing
but her own skin.

There is no kind way to tell this story,
so I may as well tell it true:
you would not wish yourself upon anyone.

& how else to explain grief
but as this mirror?

This impossible joy
that will not let you hold it.

This mirror that slips rocks
into your pocket & reminds you

everyone you love
has a river's mouth.

ANXIETY: A GHOST STORY

We have got to talk about the kids
in all those *Goosebumps* books.

For example,
if your family vacation
is to an amusement park
called HORRORLAND
and your station wagon explodes
in the parking lot upon arrival,
maybe
shrugging it off,
buying an extra-large popcorn,
and heading directly to
The Deadly Doom Slide
is not your best possible course of action.

Or
if you steal a weird camera
from your creepy neighbor's basement
and every picture you take
shows bad things happening,
like decapitation
and also Tofurkey,
and then all the bad things from the pictures
start happening,
STOP TAKING PICTURES.

Or
if you move into your new house
and there are a bunch of small children
already living in your bedroom
that your parents cannot see,
maybe

don't just grab a juice box
and go play in the cemetery
that
         is
                 in
                         your
                                 backyard.

Or
when I tell you of the ghosts
that live inside my body,

when I tell you
I have a cemetery in my backyard
and in my front yard
and in my bedroom,

when I tell you
trauma is a steep slide
you cannot see the bottom of,

that my anxiety is a camera
that shows everyone I love as bones,

when I tell you
panic is a stubborn phantom,
she will grab hold of me
and not let go for months—

this is the part of the story
when everyone is telling you to run.

To love me
is to love a haunted house.
It's fun to visit once a year,
but no one wants to live there.

When you say,
Tell me about the bad days,
it sounds like all the neighborhood kids
daring each other to ring the doorbell.

You love me
like the family
walking through Horrorland holding hands—
you are not stupid,
or careless,
or even brave.
You've just never seen
the close-up of a haunting.

Darling,
this love will not cure me.

This love will not scrape
the blood from the baseboards,
but it will turn all the lights on.

It will bring basil
back from the farmers market
and it will plant it in every windowsill.

It is the kind of love
that gives me goosebumps
when you say to the ghosts,
If you're staying,
then you better make room,

and we kiss against the walls
that tonight are not shaking,
so we turn the music up
and we dance to Miles Davis
and you say,

My god,
this house.
The way that it stands
even on the months
that no one goes into
or comes out of it.

How reckless, the way that I love
like the first chapter of a ghost story.
Like the gentlest hand
reaching out of a grave.

WHEN I SAY,
"I DON'T TRUST MYSELF AROUND YOU"

I mean
I kept the napkin
from the first time we had breakfast.

I mean
the gap in your front teeth
is the same size as the tine of a fork,
and since you left
I have been collecting cutlery.

I mean
I want to fit myself
in all your strangest places.

I mean
scrape the scorched earth
from my tongue.
Promise me again
the last time
either one of us was alone
has already come and gone.

I mean
I am sorry for the ways
we will fuck each other up.

I mean
there is ugly in me
exactly the size and shape
of your lips on my neck.

THERE ARE A LOT OF VILLAINS
IN THIS STORY,
AND MOST OF THEM ARE ME

I blame that one Nick Drake album.
Blame the missed bus.
Blame the one more drink.
Blame the way he holds his glass of wine
like a crystal ball at a county fair,
like beckon,
like look closely,
like if I squint my eyes
couldn't it be my name in his mouth?

I tell my friend on the phone,
Everything is such a mess.
She says, *Brenna, I love you,*
but look at your hands.
And I don't know how I missed it,
these fistfuls of mud,
these months finger-painting the walls,
pressing dirt
into any clean thing I could find.

& I'M SORRY
after Tara Hardy

IT FELL APART QUICKLY & I'M SORRY
[in 45 words]

with a lime
& his wrist,
three decades of salt
& my selfish tongue
taking it in.
let me show you a magic trick,
I said
(like I always say)
& then there was tom petty
& my bedroom,
& god, forgive me
for the way that I worship him.

I'M A PART SORRY
[in 26 words, taken from the original 45]

let me show you a magic trick—
his tongue,
my bedroom.
forgive me, I said
(like I always say)
& then there was god,
taking it in.

SORRY I'M APART
[& then 8 words]

forgive me my salt,
my decades of taking.

IT HAS BEEN TOO LONG SINCE ANYONE
HAS SEEN ME NAKED

who wasn't a doctor or the neighbors,
which is not a good reason to call him,

but
we quote all the same lines in all the same movies,
which is not the same thing as missing someone
but is a bad habit that will leave my voice hollow
and lacking all the months he is in some other city.

There is no love poem here.

I know
because I looked for it.

There is only the way he fills out crossword puzzles.
Adding on boxes where his answers don't fit.
There is the way he watches me watching him
like a stampede in his direction.

He touches the backs of my hands too long
when he says goodbye, and I think of the fallen tree in the side yard,
devoured by carpenter ants;
it is hollow, but you wouldn't know it from a distance.

It isn't love, my friends say gently, as if
I needed reminding. As if I could mistake
my bathtub for an ocean.

That's the point, I laugh
and gnaw against the meat of my cheek.
I know the exact ways he can hurt me.

I promised him I was done
being this boiling-over pot,

this thing that brings him running
from the other room, but
Lord, the way that he bowls.

The way he cradles the ball in both hands
before taking a long step back
and sending the whole room careening.

TODAY I AM TIRED OF BEING A WOMAN

you know that poem
about the icebox and the plums?

i've always thought
it would be nice
to be an icebox.

instead of a wanted thing.
instead of a grabbing hand.

i have practice in the art
of being cold on purpose.

how else
to keep the inside from spoiling?
to keep the rot from creeping in?

MY THERAPIST ASKS ME
TO DESCRIBE YOU

so I tell her about the house
on Amherst, the For Sale sign,
the stupid purple blinds;

tell her about that Papa Murphy's
that used to be a Blockbuster,
the way you tried to rent movies there
for like three years after
because you knew it made me laugh;

say,
have you ever come home to find the doors locked,
your key in a coat pocket on the bedroom floor,
had to break your own window with a flowerpot?

I say,
if those years were a place
they would have to be the yellow line,
an overcrowded train
hurtling in your direction;

I say,
there was not room enough
in my heart for the both of us.

Tonight
I will fall asleep next to a man I love,

which is the only thing
you and he have in common.

& what a blessing
this silly, boring love is.

the way I do not lose myself in him.

the way I am not lost at all.

I DO

after Clementine von Radics

A man who does not love me
anymore laces up his best shoes,
slides a ring onto another girl's finger.
& I eat cake by the handful,
play "The Way You Look Tonight" &
dance barefoot in the wet grass of my backyard.

& it is the most joyous occasion,
that when I said, *I will love you forever,*
I meant I will love you
until I stop loving you
& then
I will leave gently.
I will hope your next good love lasts
the rest of your life. & I do.

I do.

THE AUTHOR'S MOTHER WRITES
A GROCERY LIST

- Get an oil with a low smoke point, canola, maybe, or sunflower. *Let it pop up on your skin, remind you you've still got your hands, and bellies to feed, and babies who know nothing of your wedding vows.*

- Pick up a chicken to spatchcock. *Tell the butcher you'll cut the back-bone out yourself.*

- *If you're going to spend the week crying,* buy a crate of onions. *Might as well get a soup out of it. Might as well get to make something burn.*

- Bring home live lobsters. *Watch them give in to the boil.*

- To check the heat, press your palm hard against the stockpot. *Press your tongue back into your mouth.*

- The chicken cooks faster when you split it open and lay it flat like a book.

- The lobster tastes best with an absurd amount of lemon; the key is to squeeze until you can't imagine they could give any more, & then to just keep squeezing.

- *And isn't this what they taught us back in school?*

- *Isn't this what good wifehood looks like?*

- *A hot, hot oven with something bubbling over inside?*

- *Dinner on the table and a house of closed mouths?*

FEBRUARY

& I don't understand how people can say the word "heaven" like it isn't
a swear word. like it doesn't make my mom gasp, press her whole hand
to her mouth, & wonder who taught you to say that shit in polite com-
pany. because really, when you say *heaven*, it's just a shined-up way
of saying *not here*, so either way, we're left holding not-enough hands
and trying to remember how to set a smaller table. two weeks ago, I
got a bloody nose as the plane took off, & no one seemed to notice, so I
just shoved damp red napkins into all my pockets, and it has been like
this ever since. strangers smile at me on the street, & I want to press my
palms into their faces—*can't you see?*

Can't you see I'm bleeding on everything?

I AM NOT CLINICALLY CRAZY ANYMORE

according to the paperwork
& the new prescription.

but
there's this spot on the sidewalk
along the way to work
where for almost three months
there was this dead rat
& every time I passed it I thought,

someone should do something
about this dead rat

or

I should do something
about this dead rat

then held my breath
& kept walking.

& almost a year later
every time I pass it
I think,

that's the spot
where the dead rat
used to be.

where no one did anything
for so long.

I have not almost-killed-myself
in two years and three months,

but

I look at old poems and think,

someone should do something
about this bleeding body.

my mouth,
the space
where a dead thing used to live,

even now.

WHEN THE CRAZY CAME BACK

she didn't throw out all the dinners,
spill the wine down my boring throat.

she didn't look anything like the last time.
didn't pound the door in.

she knows this house too well by now,
knows I'll let her in by nightfall.

I could set my watch by the knocking.
I plant dahlias in spring

& come October panic blooms
in every window box, the crazy gathers it up.

washes a vase by hand.
she has learned to be a gentle houseguest.

to seal the windows up for winter.
we could almost forgive last autumn.

the pills from my dead grandmother's purse,
that man & his wedding ring,

the way the crazy called herself my name
& I almost let her keep it.

this body knows fear like a front porch
knows welcome—it is always coming home.

& you cannot pull the crazy out of me
the way you cannot put a flower back to bed,

but this body knows withstand. knows
what the morning looks like when she says *stay*.

the crazy
is a quitter.

you have a perfect
attendance record for this life.

& I will stay.
& I will stay.

ACKNOWLEDGMENTS

Thank you to:

Button Poetry, for being a platform and a springboard and a community of storytellers. Sam Cook, for convincing me this book was something worth doing. Hanif Abdurraqib, for helping me do it well. Megan, my touchstone—I will be grateful every day of my life that you decided to be my friend despite your better judgment. Melanie, without whom the poems never would have made it in the first place. Erin, and your unfailing enthusiasm and belief in each of us. Mia, my best role model of hustle and strength. Petra, my favorite form of sunshine. What a blessing it has been to learn to love each other the past ten years. Portland Poetry Slam, for raising me as a writer. Doc Luben and Clementine von Radics, for editing first drafts of many of these poems and keeping me writing. Leisure crew, for being a weekly support for so many years. Dad, for telling me that my early poems were funny. Every person at Michigan Law for teaching me how to fight for what matters and reminding me that it almost always does. Kevin & Nicole, for cheering me on and inspiring me to work harder and be my best self. Mom, I mean it. All the best parts of me are you.

ABOUT THE AUTHOR

Brenna Twohy is a storyteller and an advocate from Portland, Oregon. Her poetry has been showcased on *The Huffington Post, BuzzFeed, Mic,* and her mother's living room table. After representing Portland at the 2013, 2014, and 2016 National Poetry Slams, Brenna moved to Ann Arbor, Michigan. She is currently in her final year of law school, where she focuses on criminal justice reform and holistic defense work. She really wants you to go to jury duty.

OTHER BOOKS BY BUTTON POETRY

If you enjoyed this book, please consider checking out some of our others, below. Readers like you allow us to keep broadcasting and publishing. Thank you!

Neil Hilborn, *Our Numbered Days*
Hanif Abdurraqib, *The Crown Ain't Worth Much*
Olivia Gatwood, *New American Best Friend*
Donte Collins, *Autopsy*
Melissa Lozada-Oliva, *peluda*
Sabrina Benaim, *Depression & Other Magic Tricks*
William Evans, *Still Can't Do My Daughter's Hair*
Rudy Francisco, *Helium*
Guante, *A Love Song, A Death Rattle, A Battle Cry*
Rachel Wiley, *Nothing Is Okay*
Neil Hilborn, *The Future*
Phil Kaye, *Date & Time*
Andrea Gibson, *Lord of the Butterflies*
Blythe Baird, *If My Body Could Speak*
Desireé Dallagiacomo, *SINK*
Dave Harris, *Patricide*
Michael Lee, *The Only Worlds We Know*
Raych Jackson, *Even the Saints Audition*

Available at buttonpoetry.com/shop and more!

.